U.S.
Social Studies
Yellow Pages

for Students and Teachers

Revised Edition

from the Kids' Stuff™ People

Incentive Publications, Inc.
Nashville, Tennessee

Special acknowledgement is accorded to
- *Marjorie Frank for compiling and organizing the materials included in this publication*
- *Susan Eaddy for the cover art*
- *Jean K. Signor, Editor*

ISBN 0-86530-559-5
Library of Congress Control Number: 2001094391

PRINTED IN THE UNITED STATES OF AMERICA
www.incentivepublications.com

Table of Contents

U.S. GEOGRAPHY

SOCIAL STUDIES SKILLS CHECKLISTS

UNITED STATES HISTORY SKILLS

Major Eras & Events in U.S. History

_____ Identify and describe key events in U.S. history
_____ Explain the significance of selected events in U.S. history
_____ Recognize general time period of events in U.S. history
_____ Place major U.S. historical events on a timeline
_____ Describe and compare eras in U.S. history
_____ Place events within eras in U.S. history
_____ Recognize major conflicts in U.S. history
_____ Understand causes and results of major conflicts in U.S. history
_____ Recognize chronology of events in U.S. history
_____ Recognize and describe changes caused by historical events
_____ Identify source and importance of key quotes in U.S. history

People, Places, & Organizations in U.S. History

_____ Identify key persons in U.S. history
_____ Describe accomplishments of key persons in U.S. history
_____ Connect key persons to an era in U.S. history
_____ Recognize the state location of key events in history
_____ Identify and locate significant U.S. landmarks and monuments
_____ Associate events or issues with state, city, or regional locations
_____ Recognize the purpose of key organizations or agencies in U.S. history
_____ Identify policies and programs in U.S. history and recognize their purposes

Early U.S. History Through 1800

_____ Show understanding of the inhabitance of North America by indigenous groups
_____ Show understanding of the ways of life of the Native Americans
_____ Identify some groups of Native Americans
_____ Describe changes brought to Native American life by the coming of Europeans
_____ Identify key events and persons involved in the explorations and discoveries in North America
_____ Identify characteristics of different American colonies
_____ Describe colonial life
_____ Describe reasons why various groups came to America
_____ Recognize causes and results of the French & Indian War
_____ Recognize causes and results of the Revolutionary War
_____ Explain the significance of quotes from the Revolutionary War period
_____ Define unalienable rights
_____ Understand some challenges faced by the new government
_____ Recognize chronology of events surrounding the Revolutionary War;
place events on a timeline

19th Century U.S. History

_____ Explain significance of events in 19th century U.S. history

_____ Recognize key persons and events in the Westward Movement and expansion of the U.S. to the west; understand Manifest Destiny concept

_____ Recognize causes, results, and other factors related to the Civil War period

_____ Recognize attitude of America toward European influence; describe Monroe Doctrine

_____ Recognize causes and effects of various events in 19th century U.S. history

_____ Identify results of the War of 1812

_____ Recognize effects of the relocation of Native Americans

_____ Recognize some of the issues surrounding slavery and abolition in America

_____ Identify events, people, and changes due to the rise of industrialism in the U.S.

_____ Identify key events and issues surrounding Reconstruction

_____ Recognize results of the Spanish-American War

_____ Recognize events and issues from the Ages of Jefferson and Jackson

_____ Recognize events and issues from the Age of Reform

_____ Identify causes and results of the Mexican War

_____ Describe benefits and problems brought on by the Industrial Revolution

_____ Identify significant American inventors and inventions

Modern U.S. History Since 1900

_____ Identify key events related to modern America

_____ Describe significance of events in modern U.S. history

_____ Describe causes, results, and alliances of World War I

_____ Identify causes and outcomes from conflicts in modern U.S. history

_____ Describe features and events of the 1920s

_____ Identify causes of the Depression

_____ Describe causes, results, and alliances of World War II

_____ Identify programs of the New Deal

_____ Identify events and effects of the Cold War

_____ Identify location and results of the Korean War

_____ Identify features of the Civil Rights Movement

_____ Identify key events in post-World War II America

_____ Identify causes, issues, and events related to the Vietnam War

_____ Identify contributions of key persons in modern U.S. history

_____ Identify persons, achievements, and events related to U.S. space exploration

_____ Recognize chronology of events in modern U.S. history

U.S. Social Studies Yellow Pages, Rev. Ed.

UNITED STATES GOVERNMENT & CITIZENSHIP SKILLS

Key U.S. Documents

_____ Recognize the purposes and names of key U.S. documents

_____ Discriminate between important U.S. documents

_____ Understand concepts covered in key U.S. documents

_____ Recognize key ideas of the Declaration of Independence

_____ Recognize key ideas of the Bill of Rights (and their meaning and importance)

_____ Recognize the significance of the Constitution and its various articles

_____ Discriminate between parts of the Constitution; identify purposes of each section

_____ Identify the significance of key amendments to the Constitution

Government Structure & Function

_____ Show understanding of structure of the federal government

_____ Identify and explain some principles of democracy and representative government

_____ Distinguish between the duties of the three branches of government

_____ Explain the concept of separation of powers

_____ Identify duties and requirements of the executive, legislative, and judicial branches

_____ Describe members and duties of the President's Cabinet

_____ Recognize process by which a law is made; understand how a veto can be overridden

_____ Identify some key Supreme Court decisions in U.S. history

_____ Distinguish between different kinds of powers: enumerated, implied, inherent, reserved, concurrent, delegated, reserved; identify powers that are federal, state, or shared

_____ Show understanding of election processes

Officials, Agencies, & Institutions

_____ Recognize responsibilities of different officials of the government

_____ Identify some U.S. presidents and events that took place during their administrations

_____ Identify government officials of state and local governments

_____ Identify some key institutions and their functions

_____ Show understanding of some of the principles upon which the U.S. government is based

_____ Identify the names and functions of key government agencies

U.S. Citizenship

_____ Identify current government officials at the federal and local level

_____ Identify significant events, issues, officials, and locations in the history of one's own state

_____ Show understanding of voting rights and the voting process

_____ Show understanding of some responsibilities of citizens

_____ Identify some rights and responsibilities of officials in relationship to elections

_____ Show understanding and recognition of national symbols

_____ Recognize some of the workings of the U.S. economic system

_____ Describe some uses of taxes

UNITED STATES GEOGRAPHY SKILLS

Geographical Features

_____ Identify different kinds of landforms in the U.S.

_____ Identify different kinds of water bodies within the U.S.

_____ Compare sizes and other characteristics of landforms and water bodies

_____ Recognize geographical features of different U.S. regions

_____ Locate and describe major climate patterns and zones of the U.S.

_____ Identify factors that affect climate

_____ Describe wind patterns and ocean currents that affect U.S. climate

U.S. Regions

_____ Identify the major U.S. regional divisions and identify the states in them

_____ Identify resources, products, and features associated with specific Regions

_____ Identify resources, products, and features of the Pacific Region

_____ Identify resources, products, and features of the Mountain Region

_____ Identify resources, products, and features of the Plains Region

_____ Identify resources, products, and features of the Southwest Region

_____ Identify resources, products, and features of the Great Lakes Region

_____ Identify resources, products, and features of the Southeast Region

_____ Identify resources, products, and features of the Middle Atlantic Region

_____ Identify resources, products, and features of the New England Region

Important Places & Spaces

_____ Locate the United States and its neighbors on a world map

_____ Recognize and compare the locations of states

_____ Identify locations of important bodies of water in the U.S.

_____ Identify state locations of major U.S. cities

_____ Recognize state locations of major geographic features

_____ Recognize and locate major cities in relation to other cities and features

_____ Identify locations and significance of national parks and monuments

_____ Identify locations and significance of key cultural and human-made features in the U.S.

_____ Locate other North American, Central American, and South American countries

_____ Identify key physical and cultural features of neighboring countries to the U.S.

Human Geography

_____ Identify the human characteristics of different regions or states

_____ Recognize reasons why people live differently in different places

_____ Recognize cultural traditions and behaviors that differ from location to location

_____ Identify different economic bases for different areas

_____ Show an understanding of population distribution across the U.S.

_____ Recognize differing characteristics of rural and urban areas

_____ Give examples of ways human life has been shaped or changed by the physical geography of the places they live

MAP SKILLS

Map Tools & Resources

_____ Distinguish between different kinds of maps

_____ Understand and use the concept of scale on a map

_____ Identify parts of a map and their purposes

_____ Read and use a map key

_____ Understand the use of symbols on a map

_____ Choose the best title for a map

_____ Identify the world hemispheres

_____ Recognize the major lines of latitude and the poles

_____ Use a grid to locate features on a map

_____ Place features on a grid map

Directions, Distances, & Locations

_____ Use scale to determine distances on maps

_____ Find directions on maps of areas within the U.S.

_____ Identify and compare U.S. locations

_____ Find locations using lines of latitude and longitude

_____ Identify and locate countries and cities in the U.S. and neighboring countries

_____ Use latitude and longitude to locate cities and features in the U.S.

Finding Information on Maps

_____ Find information on a road map

_____ Find information on a political map

_____ Find information on an elevation map

_____ Find information on a population map

_____ Find information of a product map

_____ Use a time zone map to find information and solve problems

_____ Find information on a weather map

U.S. HISTORY & GOVERNMENT

JUST THE FACTS

Capital: — Washington, D. C.

Form of Government: — Republic

Area: — 3,618,770 square miles

Elevation

Highest: — Mt. McKinley (Denali) in Alaska, 20,320 ft. (6,194 m.) above sea level.

Lowest: — In Death Valley in California, 282 ft. (86 m.) below sea level.

Physical Features

Longest river: — Mississippi (2,340 miles)

Largest lake within the U.S.: — Lake Michigan (22,300 sq. mi.)

Largest island: — Hawaii (4,038 sq. mi.)

Population, 2000 Census: — 281,421,906

Religions: — no official religion (some examples: Protestant, Roman Catholic, Jewish, other)

Chief Products

Agriculture: — beef cattle, chickens, corn, cotton, eggs, hogs, milk, soybeans, wheat

Fishing industry: — crabs, salmon, shrimp

Manufacturing & Technology: — airplanes, broadcasting equipment, cameras, computers and computer parts, fabricated metal products, gasoline, guided missiles, industrial chemicals, industrial machinery, motor vehicles, paper, pharmaceuticals, plastics, printed materials, processed foods, steel, various other kinds of small and large electronic equipment

Mining: — coal, natural gas, petroleum

Flag: — Adopted June 14, 1777

Motto: — "In God We Trust," adopted July 30, 1956

National Anthem: — "The Star-Spangled Banner," adopted March 3, 1931

Bird: — Bald eagle, adopted June 20, 1782

Flower: — Rose, adopted October 7, 1986

Money: — Basic Unit—dollar

ADVENTURES TO AMERICA

Date	Explorer	Nationality	Discovery or Area of Exploration
1492	Christopher Columbus	Italian	Bahamas, Cuba, Hispaniola
1513	Juan Ponce de Leon	Spanish	Florida
1519	Alonso de Piñeda	Spanish	Mouth of the Mississippi River
1524	Giovanni da Verrazano	Italian-French	Atlantic coast and New York Harbor
1536	A.N. Cabeza de Vaca	Spanish	Texas coast and interior
1539	Francisco de Ulloa	Spanish	California coast
1539–41	Hernando de Soto	Spanish	Mississippi River, near Memphis
1539	Marcos de Niza	Spanish	Southwest U.S.
1540	Francisco V. de Coronado	Spanish	Southwest U.S.
1540	Hernando Alarcon	Spanish	Colorado River
1540	Garcia Lopez de Cardenas	Spanish	Grand Canyon and the Colorado River
1542	Juan Rodriguez Cabrillo	Portuguese-Spanish	San Diego harbor
1565	Pedro Menendez	Spanish	St. Augustine
1577–80	Francis Drake	English	California coast
1582	Antonio de Espejo	Spanish	Southwest (now New Mexico)
1584	Amadas & Barlow (for Sir Walter Raleigh)	English	Virginia
1585–87	Sir Walter Raleigh's men	English	Roanoke Island, North Carolina

Date	Explorer	Nationality	Discovery or Area of Exploration
1595	Sir Walter Raleigh	English	Orinoco River in South America
1607	Capt. John Smith	English	Atlantic coast
1609–10	Henry Hudson	English-Dutch	Hudson River, Hudson Bay
1634	Jean Nicolet	French	Lake Michigan and Wisconsin
1659	Pierre Esprit Radisson	French	Lake Superior and northern Mississippi River
1673	Jacques Marquette *(with Louis Jolliet)*	French	Upper Mississippi River to Arkansas
1678–87	Sieur Duluth	French	Lake Superior region
1679–82	Sieur de Henri de Tonti *(with LaSalle)*	French	Great Lakes region and Mississippi River
1680	Louis Hennepin	Belgian	Upper Mississippi River region
1682	Sieur de La Salle	French	Mississippi River to Gulf of Mexico
1789	David Thompson	Canadian	Western Canada
1789	Alexander Mackenzie	Canadian	Canadian Northwest
1804–06	William Clark and Meriwether Lewis	American	Led expedition across the Rocky Mountains to the Pacific Ocean
1805–07	Zebulon Pike	American	Middle West and Rocky Mountains
1824–25	James Bridger	American	Great Salt Lake
1824–29	Jedediah Strong Smith	American	Great Basin region, Rocky Mountains to California and Pacific Northwest
1842–46	John Charles Fremont	American	American West

THE FIRST AMERICANS

THE EASTERN WOODLANDS

Major Tribes of the Northeast

Abnaki
Delaware
Erie
Fox
Huron
Illinois
Iroquois:
- Cayuga
- Mohawk
- Onandaga
- Oneida
- Seneca

Kickapoo
Mahican
Malecite
Massachusetts
Menominee
Miami
Mohegan
Narraganset
Ojibwa
Potawatomi
Sauk
Susquehanna
Wampanoag
Winnebago

Major Tribes of the Southeast

Calusa
Cherokee
Chickasaw
Chitimaca
Choctaw
Creek
Natchez
Powhatan
Seminole
Shawnee
Timucua
Tuscarora
Yamasee
Yuchi

THE PLAINS

Arapaho
Arikara
Assiniboin
Atakapa
Blackfoot:
- Blood
- Piegan
- Brea

Caddo
Cheyenne
Comanche
CreeCrow
Gros Ventre
Hidatsa
Iowa
Kansa
Karankawa
Kiowa
Mandan
Missouri
Nez Perce
Omaha
Osage
Oto
Pawnee
Ponca
Quapaw
Shoshone
Sioux:
- Ogalala
- Santee
- Sisseton
- Teton
- Yankton

Ute
Wichita

THE FAR NORTH AREA

Algonquin
Beaver
Beathuk
Carrier
Chilcotin
Cree
Dogrib
Hare
Kaska
Koyukon
Kutchin
Micmac
Montagnais
Naskapi
Ojibwa
Ottawa
Sarsi
Slave
Tanaina
Tutchone
Yellowknife

THE CALIFORNIA-INTER-MOUNTAIN AREA

Bannock
Cayuse
Chumash
Flathead
Gosiute
Hupa
Karok
Klamath
Kutenal
Luiseno
Maidu
Modoc
Mohave
Nez Percé
Paiute
Pomo
Shoshoni
Ute
Wintun
Yuki

THE NORTHWEST COAST AREA

Bella Coola
Chinook
Haida
Klikitat
Kwakiutl
Makah
Nootka
Quileute
Quinault
Tilamook
Tlingit
Tsimshian

THE SOUTHWEST AREA

Apache
Cochimi
Navaho
Paiute
Papago
Pima
Pueblo:

    Acoma
    Hopi
    Laguna
    San Ildefonso

Taos
Zia
Zuni
Serrano
Waiguri
Yakima
Yaqui
Yuma

A BAKER'S DOZEN
(The Original 13 Colonies)

New England Colonies

Colony	Year Founded	Founder	Reason for Founding	Religion	Government	Chief Trade or Crops
Massachusetts	1620	Pilgrims led by William Bradford; Puritans led by John Winthrop	religious freedom	Puritan	governor, appointed by the king	fish, lumber, shipbuilding
New Hampshire	1623	the colonists who left Massachusetts	religious freedom; profit and trade	several	governor, appointed by the king	fish, molasses
Rhode Island	1636	Roger Williams	religious freedom	several	elected by colonists	fish, lumber
Connecticut	1636	Thomas Hooker	religious and political freedom	several	elected by colonists	fish, lumber, shipbuilding

Middle Colonies

Colony	Year Founded	Founder	Reason for Founding	Religion	Government	Chief Trade or Crops
New York [New Amsterdam]	1626	Dutch	to expand trade	Dutch Reformed, others	governor, appointed by the king	shipbuilding, trade
New Jersey	1664	Lord John Berkeley; Sir George Carteret	religious and political freedom; investment	Quaker, Dutch Reformed, others	governor, appointed by the king	rye, oats, wheat
Pennsylvania	1681	William Penn	religious and political freedom; investment	Quaker	governor, selected by proprietor	trade, shipbuilding
Delaware	1682	William Penn	to expand trade	Quaker	governor, selected by proprietor	tobacco

Southern Colonies

Colony	Year Founded	Founder	Reason for Founding	Religion	Government	Chief Trade or Crops
Virginia	1607	John Smith	trade and agriculture	Anglican	governor, appointed by the king	tobacco
Maryland	1634	Lord Baltimore	religious and political freedom; investment	Catholic, Protestant	governor, selected by proprietor	tobacco
North Carolina	1654	Virginia settlers	religious freedom; to profit from trade and agriculture	several	governor, appointed by the king	rice, tobacco, pine tar, pitch
South Carolina	1663	English	religious freedom; to profit from trade and agriculture	several	governor, appointed by the king	rice, tobacco, pine tar, pitch
Georgia	1732	James Oglethorpe	haven for debtors; investment	Baptist; others	governor, appointed by the king	tobacco

"WE, THE PEOPLE . . ."

ARTICLES OF CONFEDERATION

The agreement under which the thirteen original colonies established a government of state in 1781; served as the basic law of the new nation until the present U.S. Constitution went into effect in 1789.

13th AMENDMENT to the CONSTITUTION

Ratified in 1865; outlawed slavery within the United States or any place subject to the jurisdiction of the U.S.

15th AMENDMENT to the CONSTITUTION

Ratified in 1870; stated that the right of a citizen of the United States to vote could not be denied because of race or color or previous condition of slavery.

19th AMENDMENT to the CONSTITUTION

Ratified in 1920; stated that the right of a citizen of the United States to vote could not be denied on account of gender.

BILL OF RIGHTS

The first ten Amendments to the United States Constitution, which were proposed on September 25, 1789, and became law on December 15, 1791; describes the fundamental liberties of the people and forbids the government to violate these rights.

CIVIL RIGHTS ACT OF 1866

A law that made blacks citizens of the United States and forbade the southern states from restricting the rights of freed slaves with special laws. This law was passed when Congress overrode President Johnson's veto.

CIVIL RIGHTS ACT OF 1964

A law that prohibited racial discrimination in public facilities of all sorts. It also made registration and voting safer and easier for southern blacks

COMPROMISE OF 1850

A series of acts passed in 1850, by which the United States Congress hoped to settle the strife between Northern opponents of slavery and Southern slave-owners; helped delay civil war for about ten years.

CONSTITUTION OF THE UNITED STATES

The supreme law of the land, ratified in 1788; established the form of the United States government and the rights and liberties of the American people. The Constitution consists of a preamble, seven articles, and twenty-six amendments.

DECLARATION OF INDEPENDENCE

A statement setting forth the colonists' reasons for declaring their independence from Great Britain; July 4, 1776.

U.S. Social Studies Yellow Pages, Rev. Ed.

EMANCIPATION PROCLAMATION

Issued by President Abraham Lincoln on January 1, 1863, during the Civil War; declared all slaves free.

THE FEDERALIST

The collective title of a series of eighty-five letters written to newspapers during 1787 and 1788 by Alexander Hamilton, James Madison, and John Jay, urging ratification of the Constitution.

GETTYSBURG ADDRESS

A short speech delivered by Abraham Lincoln on November 19, 1863, at the site of the Battle of Gettysburg; part of ceremonies dedicating a portion of the battlefield as a cemetery for those who had died in this battle.

HOMESTEAD ACT

Passed by Congress in May, 1862; provided that any person over 21 years of age (head of family and a citizen, or one intending to become a citizen) could obtain title to 160 acres of public land if he or she lived on the land and improved it for five years, or the settler could pay $1.25 an acre.

KANSAS-NEBRASKA ACT

Passed by Congress in 1854; provided that two new territories, Kansas and Nebraska, were to be established on the Indian land that lay west of the bend of the Missouri River and north of 37 degrees north latitude.

MAYFLOWER COMPACT

The first agreement for self-government ever enacted in America; forty-one male adults aboard the Mayflower signed the compact and set up a government in Plymouth Colony.

MISSOURI COMPROMISE

Adopted by Congress in March, 1820; admitted Maine as a free state and Missouri as a slave state into the Union.

MONROE DOCTRINE

Set forth by President James Monroe in a message to Congress on December 2, 1823; practically guaranteed all the independent nations of the Western Hemisphere against European control and/or interference.

NORTHWEST ORDINANCE

Passed by U. S. Congress on July 13, 1787; provided for the government of the region north of the Ohio River and west of Pennsylvania, then called the Northwest Territory; became a model for all territories that later entered the Union as states.

THE BIG THREE BRANCHES

THE EXECUTIVE BRANCH

The President: the nation's chief executive
The Vice President

Executive Offices of the President
    Council of Economic Advisers
    Office of Management and Budget
    National Security Council
    White House Office
    Office of Policy Development
    Office of the U.S. Trade Representative
    Council on Environmental Quality
    Office of Science and Technology Policy
    Office of Administration

Executive Departments
    Department of Agriculture
    Department of Commerce
    Department of Defense
    Department of Education
    Department of Energy
    Department of Health and Human Services
    Department of Housing and Urban Development
    Department of the Interior
    Department of Justice
    Department of Labor
    Department of State
    Department of Transportation
    Department of the Treasury

THE LEGISLATIVE BRANCH

Congress of the United States
    House of Representatives
    Senate
General Accounting Office
Government Printing Office
Library of Congress
Architect of the Capitol
United States Botanic Garden
Office of Technology Assessment
Congressional Budget Office
Copyright Royalty Tribunal

THE JUDICIAL BRANCH

Supreme Court of the United States
Courts of Appeals
Court of Appeals for the Federal Circuit
Court of Claims
Court of International Trade
Court of Military Appeals
District Courts
Territorial Courts
Tax Court
Administrative Office of the United States Courts
Federal Judicial Center

U.S. Social Studies Yellow Pages, Rev. Ed.

THE STORY OF "OLD GLORY"

"The Stars and Stripes" is the popular name for the red, white, and blue United States national flag. Francis Scott Key first called this flag the "Star-Spangled Banner" in 1814 when he wrote the poem that later became the national anthem. A sea captain from Massachusetts, William Driver, gave the name "Old Glory" to the United States flag in 1824.

The "Stars and Stripes" represents the land, the people, the government, and the ideals of the United States, no matter when or where it is displayed. The stars, stripes, and colors of the national flag appear in many federal and state flags.

There is no record that explains why the colors red, white, and blue were chosen for the flag; however, the resolution on the Great Seal of the United States lists meanings for these colors. Red stands for hardiness and courage, white for purity and innocence, and blue for vigilance, perseverance, and justice. The stripes in the flag represent the thirteen original colonies.

A resolution passed by Congress in 1777 stated that the flag should have 13 stars. Congress, however, did not specify how the stars should be arranged. Various presidents sometimes proclaimed new arrangements for the stars when a new state entered the Union.

FAMOUS FIRST FLIGHTS OF THE STARS AND STRIPES

August 16, 1777 — in the land Battle of Bennington on the New York-Vermont border

November 1, 1777 — on a U.S. Navy ship, Ranger, when John Paul Jones left Portsmouth, New Hampshire

December 2, 1777 — in a foreign port when John Paul Jones arrived on the Ranger

Year 1784 — in the Pacific Ocean, when the EMPRESS OF CHINA sailed to Macao

September 30, 1787, to August 10, 1790 — when the COLUMBIA sailed around the world

May, 1812 — over a schoolhouse in Massachusetts

Year 1840 — in Antarctica on the FLYING FISH expedition of Charles Wilkes

Year 1861 — at a Flag Day celebration in Connecticut

July 20, 1969 — on the moon when crew members Neil Armstrong and Edwin Aldrin, Jr., landed and disembarked the APOLLO 11 spacecraft

Twelve Flag Terms To Know:

badge — an emblem or design, usually on the fly

battle flag — carried by armed forces on land

bunting — cloth decorated with stripes of the national colors

canton — the upper corner of a flag where a special design appears

color — a special flag carried by a military unit or officer

field — the background color of a flag

fly — the free end of a flag, farthest from the staff

halyard — a rope used to hoist and lower a flag

national flag — the flag of a country

pennant — a triangular or tapering flag

staff — the pole on which the flag hangs

standard — a flag around which people rally

SYMBOLS OF FREEDOM

AMERICAN EAGLE

The United States chose the bald eagle as its national bird in 1782. The bald eagle has powerful wings, and its white head feathers give it the appearance of baldness. Its tail is also white.

THE GREAT SEAL OF THE UNITED STATES

A chief symbol of the nation used on official documents. Adopted by the Continental Congress on June 20, 1782. The elements of the seal are derived from many sources. The eagle is a symbol of sovereignty. The olive branch stands for peace, and the arrows stand for war. The constellation symbolizes the nation as a sovereign republic. The color red stands for hardiness and valor; blue for justice, vigilance, and perseverance; and white for purity and innocence. The pyramid represents strength. The Great Seal is kept in the United States Department of State.

LIBERTY BELL

The Liberty Bell is a symbol of American independence. The bell was originally made in England in 1752 and was later sent to the State House in Philadelphia, Pennsylvania. It broke after its arrival and was recast in Philadelphia. The bell was rung on July 8, 1776, along with other church bells, to announce the adoption of the Declaration of Independence. The Liberty Bell was rung each year until 1835, when it cracked as it was ringing during the funeral of Chief Justice John Marshall. The bell is no longer rung; it is now housed in Liberty Bell Pavilion, just north of Independence Hall in Philadelphia.

THE 4th of JULY

July fourth is regularly celebrated as a day to honor and remember American independence and the events that made it possible. July fourth is the anniversary of the first announcement that the Declaration of Independence was adopted.

THE PLEDGE OF ALLEGIANCE

The pledge (to the flag) is a promise of allegiance to the United States. Public school students first recited it in 1892. Francis Bellamy of Boston wrote the original pledge. In 1942 Congress made the pledge part of its code for use of the flag. The pledge is as follows:

"I pledge allegiance to the flag
of the United States of America
and to the Republic for which it stands,
one Nation under God, indivisible,
with Liberty and Justice for all."

U.S. Social Studies Yellow Pages, Rev. Ed.

"THE STAR-SPANGLED BANNER"

This is the national anthem of the United States. It was inspired by the United States flag during the War of 1812. The song was written (as a poem) by Francis Scott Key. Its music was later composed by John Stafford Smith. Congress officially approved the song as the national anthem in March, 1931. The song has four verses, but ordinarily, only the first verse is used:

O say, can you see, by the dawn's early light,

What so proudly we hailed at the twilight's last gleaming?

Whose broad stripes and bright stars, through the perilous fight,

O'er the ramparts we watched, were so gallantly streaming!

And the rockets' red glare, the bombs bursting in air,

Gave proof through the night that our flag was still there:

O say, does that star-spangled banner yet wave

O'er the land of the free and the home of the brave?

STATUE OF LIBERTY

The Statue of Liberty is a large copper statue, which faces the channel of New York harbor. It is a symbol of American liberty under a free form of government and one of the largest statues ever made. Frederic Auguste Bartholdi, a French sculptor, designed the statue and supervised its construction. France presented the monument to the United States in 1884 as a symbol of friendship, and in commemoration of the two countries' alliance during the American Revolution.

The statue's title is "Liberty Enlightening the World". It has become a symbol of freedom for oppressed people everywhere.

Famous Facts About the Statue of Liberty

- Height: 151 ft., 1 in. Stands on a granite and concrete pedestal located on Liberty Island

- Weight: 450,000 pounds

- Torch: 305 ft., 1 in. above the base of the pedestal; shines through leaded glass; illuminated with 14 lamps (14,000 watts)

- Crown: 25-window observation platform accommodating as many as 30 visitors at one time

- Interior: Two parallel stairways, each with 168 steps

AMERICAN CHRONOLOGY

The following are some important dates and events in American history.

1607 Founding of Jamestown, the first permanent British settlement in North America

1619 Establishment in Virginia of the House of Burgesses, the first representative legislature in America

1620 Pilgrims founded Plymouth Colony

1624 Dutch established the settlement of New Netherland

1626 Peter Minuit bought Manhattan for the Dutch from Manahat Indians, paying trinkets worth $24

1634 Maryland founded as Catholic colony with religious tolerance

1636 The first college in the colonies was founded (Harvard)
Roger Williams founded Providence, Rhode Island

1638 Swedes established settlement of New Sweden

1647 Massachusetts established first colonial public school system

1660 British Parliament passed Navigation Act

1664 England took control of New Netherland and New Sweden

1676 Indian war in New England ended August 12

1683 William Penn signed treaty with Delaware Indians and paid for Pennsylvania lands

1699 French settlements established in Mississippi and Louisiana

1704 The first successful colonial newspaper, The Boston Newsletter, began publication

1716 First theater in colonies opened in Williamsburg, Virginia

1732 Benjamin Franklin published first POOR RICHARD'S ALMANAC

1741 Captain Vitus Bering, a Dane employed by the Russians, reached Alaska

1752 Benjamin Franklin flew a homemade kite during a storm to prove that lightning is a form of electricity

1756 A stagecoach line linked New York City and Philadelphia

1757 The first street lights in the colonies were erected in Philadelphia

1763 Britain defeated France in the French and Indian War and gained control of eastern North America

1764 Sugar Act placed duties on lumber, foodstuffs, molasses, and rum in the colonies

1765 The British Parliament passed the Stamp Act, taxing newspapers, legal documents, and other printed matter in the colonies

1767 Townsend Acts levied taxes on glass, painter's lead, paper, and tea

1770 British troops killed American civilians in the Boston Massacre

1773 Colonists staged the Boston Tea Party, dumping British tea into Boston Harbor

1774 The Intolerable Acts closed Boston Harbor and took other steps to punish colonists

The First Continental Congress met to consider action against the British

Rhode Island abolished slavery

1775 The Revolutionary War began between the colonists and the British

Patrick Henry addressed the Virginia convention, declaring, "Give me liberty or give me death."

Paul Revere and William Dawes alerted patriots that British soldiers were on their way to Concord

1776 Colonists adopted the Declaration of Independence and formed the United States of America

Nathan Hale was executed by British as spy on September 22

Continental Congress adopted Stars and Stripes as national flag

Articles of Confederation and Perpetual Union were adopted by Continental Congress

1780 Benedict Arnold named as traitor September 23

1781 Americans defeated British at Yorktown in last major battle of Revolutionary War

1783 Treaty of Paris officially ended Revolutionary War and recognized the U.S. as an independent nation

1787 Founding Fathers wrote the Constitution

1789 George Washington chosen President

1790s The first U.S. political parties developed

1791 Bill of Rights became law December 15

1793 Eli Whitney developed a toothed cotton gin

1800 Washington, D.C., became the national capital

1803 Louisiana Purchase almost doubled the size of the U.S.

1804 Lewis and Clark expedition ordered by President Jefferson

1807 Robert Fulton made the first practical steamboat trip

1811 Work began on the National Road, which would link the East and the Midwest

1812–14 The United States and Great Britain fought the War of 1812

1814 Francis Scott Key wrote "The Star-Spangled Banner."

1819 Spain surrendered Florida to U.S. February 22

1820 The Missouri Compromise ended a slavery dispute

1823 The Monroe Doctrine warned Europeans against interference in Western Hemisphere affairs

1825 The Erie Canal opened, providing a water route from the Atlantic Ocean to the Great Lakes

1830 The nation's first commercial steam locomotive, the TOM THUMB, operated in Baltimore

1832 Black Hawk War (Illinois and Wisconsin) April-September

1834 Cyrus McCormick patented the reaper

1836 Texans attacked by Mexicans at the Alamo in San Antonio

Texas independence declared March 2

1837 Samuel F. B. Morse demonstrated the first successful telegraph in the U.S.

1841 First wagon train bound for California departed Independence, Missouri, on May 1

1842 Oregon Trail opened the way for settlement of Oregon

1845 Congress admitted Texas to Union December 29

1846 Britain surrendered the southern part of the Oregon Country to the United States

1848 New territory in the West was gained as a result of U.S. victory in the Mexican War

Gold Rush began in California

1850 California was admitted to the Union September 9

The Compromise of 1850 temporarily ended a national crisis over the issue of slavery

1852 UNCLE TOM'S CABIN, by Harriet Beecher Stowe, was published

1854 Kansas-Nebraska Act was passed, leading to turmoil over issue of slavery

1856 First American kindergarten opened in Watertown, Wisconsin

1857 Dred Scott decision by U.S. Supreme Court March 6

1860 Pony Express riders began carrying mail from St. Joseph, Missouri, to the Far West.

Abraham Lincoln, a Republican, was elected President

1861–65 The Civil War was fought between the North and South

1862 Homestead Act was approved May 20

1863 Emancipation Proclamation declared freedom for all slaves in Confederate-held territory.

Lincoln read his Gettysburg Address November 19

1865 The 13th Amendment outlawed slavery throughout the United States.

Robert E. Lee surrendered to Grant at Appomattox Court House, Virginia, April 9

President Lincoln was shot by John Wilkes Booth in Ford's Theater, Washington, D.C.

1866 Ku Klux Klan formed secretly in South

1867 United States bought Alaska from Russia

1868 House of Representatives impeached President Andrew Johnson, but Senate did not remove him from office

1869 Transcontinental railroad completed

Women's suffrage law passed in Territory of Wyoming, December 10

1871 Great fire destroyed Chicago, October 8–11

1872 Congress founded Yellowstone, the first national park, in Wyoming

1875 Congress passed Civil Rights Act on March 1

1876 Alexander Graham Bell invented the telephone

1877 Thomas Edison invented the phonograph

1879 Edison invented the electric light

1884 Construction of the world's first skyscraper was begun in Chicago

1886 The American Federation of Labor was founded

1890 Ellis Island opened December 31

1898 The U. S. defeated Spain in the Spanish-American War

1903 The Wright Brothers made the first successful airplane flight at Kitty Hawk, North Carolina

1910 Boy Scouts of America founded February 8

1911 First transcontinental airplane flight

1913 The 16th Amendment gave the federal government the power to levy an income tax

1914 World War I began in Europe

1917 The United States entered World War I

1920 The 18th Amendment, prohibited the sale of alcoholic beverages nationwide

The 19th Amendment gave women complete suffrage

1923 First sound-on-film motion picture shown

1925 The Scopes Trial in Dayton, Tennessee, upheld the right of a state to ban the teaching of evolution in public schools

The Golden Age of radio broadcasting began

1927 THE JAZZ SINGER (first successful motion-picture "talkie") appeared

1929 The stock market crash brought financial ruin to thousands of investors

1930s United States suffered the Great Depression

1931 Empire State Building opened in New York City on May 1

1933 President Franklin D. Roosevelt began the New Deal program in an effort to end the Depression

1937 Amelia Earhart, aviator, and Fred Noonan, co-pilot, were lost July 2, somewhere in the Pacific

1939 New York World's Fair opened April 30

1941 Japan attacked Pearl Harbor, Hawaii, December 7

The United States entered World War II

1944 U.S. Allied forces invaded Europe at Normandy on June 6

1945 U.S. dropped the first atomic bombs used in warfare on Hiroshima and Nagasaki, Japan

U.S. became a charter member of the United Nations

1947 President Truman announced the Truman Doctrine, which pledged American aid to nations threatened by Communism

Jackie Robinson, the first black man to play in major league baseball, joined Brooklyn Dodgers April 11

1950s Television became part of most American homes

1950–53 The United States fought in the Korean War

1954 The first atomic-powered submarine, the Nautilis, was launched at Groton, Connecticut, January 21

The Supreme Court ruled unconstitutional compulsory segregation in public schools

1955 Martin Luther King, Jr., began organizing a movement to protest discrimination against blacks

1957 The Soviet Union launched SPUTNIK I, the first space satellite

1958 EXPLORER I, the first U.S. earth satellite to go into orbit, was launched by the Army in Florida January 31

First domestic jet airline passenger service in U.S.

1959 Alaska admitted to Union as 49th state January 3

Hawaii admitted as 50th state August 21

1961 Invasion of Cuba's "Bay of Pigs" April 17

Astronaut Alan B. Shepard, Jr., became the first American in space

1962 The Soviet Union removed missiles from Cuba, ending an imminent threat of war with the U.S.

Lt. Col. John H. Glenn, Jr., became first American to orbit earth February 20

James Meredith became the first black student to attend University of Mississippi October 1

1963 President John F. Kennedy was assassinated November 22

1964 Congress passed a flood of civil rights legislation

1965 American combat troops entered the Vietnam War

1968 Martin Luther King, Jr., was assassinated April 4

Senator Robert F. Kennedy was assassinated June 5

1969 Astronaut Neil Armstrong became the first person to set foot on the moon

1971 A Constitutional amendment lowering the voting age to 18 was approved by the Senate

1973 U.S. removed last ground troops from Vietnam

1974 President Richard M. Nixon became the first American president to resign
from office

1975 Vietnam War ended

1976 The U.S. celebrated its bicentennial

1986 U.S. spacecraft CHALLENGER exploded, killing all seven crew members

1987 U.S. celebrated the bicentennial of the signing of the U.S. Constitution
Public hearings began on the Iran-Contra Affair
Reagan and Gorbachev signed a pact to disarm missiles

1989 The *Exxon Valdez* caused history's largest oil spill into Alaska's Prince William Sound
U.S. troops invaded Panama to overthrow Manuel Noriega
62 deaths resulted from a major earthquake in the San Francisco area on Oct. 17
The Americans with Disabilities Act outlawed discrimination against
the handicapped
Operation Desert Storm began following Iraq's invasion of Kuwait

1991 U.S. and European allies attacked Iraq, beginning the Persian Gulf War

1992 Major riots broke out in Los Angeles, following the acquittal of 4 white policemen
whose beating of Rodney King, an African American, was caught on videotape
U.S. forces left the Philippines, after almost 100 years of presence there

1993 Federal agents raided cult Branch Davidian headquarters in Waco, Texas; 70 cult
members and 6 federal agents were killed in the raid
The World Trade Center in New York City was bombed on Feb. 26
U.S. troops joined a peacekeeping force in Bosnia

1994 51 people died in a major earthquake in Los Angeles on Jan 17
NAFTA (North American Free Trade Agreement) took effect Jan. 1

1995 A truck bomb exploded outside a federal building in Oklahoma City, killing 168
U.S. reestablished diplomatic relations with Vietnam

1996 Madeleine Albright was appointed the first female U.S. Secretary of State

1998 House of Representatives voted to impeach President Clinton
U.S. and Russia launched first components of an international space station

1999 U.S. eased restrictions on Cuba

2000 George W. Bush was declared winner of the contested presidential race after the
Supreme Court stopped the recount of votes
One American and two Russians moved into the new international space station
Government and representatives of a private company announced the completion
of the mapping of DNA sequence of the human genome

2001 A Chinese jet and a U.S. surveillance plane collided near China; the damaged U.S.
plane landed on a Chinese military base
Terrorists attacked the U.S., crashing 4 airliners at the World Trade Center
Towers in New York, the Pentagon in Washington D.C., and in rural Pennsylvania

IN DEFENSE OF FREEDOM

AMERICA AT WAR, IN CONFLICT

1775–1781	American Revolution	1914–1918	World War I
1812–1815	War of 1812	1939–1945	World War II
1846–1848	Mexican War	1950–1953	Korean War
1861–1865	Civil War	1957–1975	Vietnam War
1898	Spanish-American War	1990–1991	Persian Gulf War

BRANCHES OF THE MILITARY

DEPARTMENT OF DEFENSE

Secretary of Defense
Deputy Secretary
Executive Secretary
Assistant Secretaries of Defense

Inspector General for Defense Intelligence
Chairman, Joint Chiefs of Staff
NATO Affairs
General Council

DEPARTMENT OF THE ARMY

Secretary of the Army
Under Secretary
Assistant Secretaries
Chief of Public Affairs
Chief of Staff
General Counsel
Comptroller of the Army

Surgeon General
Adjutant General
Inspector General
Judge Advocate General
Deputy Chiefs of Staff
Assistant Chief of Staff, Intelligence
Commanders

DEPARTMENT OF THE NAVY

Secretary of the Navy
Under Secretary
Assistant Secretaries
Judge Advocate General
Chief of Naval Operations
Chief of Naval Material
Chief of Information

Surgeon General
Naval Military Personnel Command
Military Sealift Command
Chief of Naval Personnel
Commandants, Naval Bases
Commandant

DEPARTMENT OF THE AIR FORCE

Secretary of the Air Force
Under Secretary
Assistant Secretaries
General Counsel
Public Affairs
Director of Space Systems

Chief of Staff
Surgeon General
Judge Advocate
Inspector General
Deputy Chiefs of Staff
Major Air Commands

U.S. Social Studies Yellow Pages, Rev. Ed.

SOME SIGHTS TO SEE

NATIONAL MEMORIALS — *Location*

Arkansas Post	Arkansas
Arlington House	Virginia
Chamizal	Texas
Coronado	Arizona
De Soto	Florida
Federal Hall	New York
Fort Caroline	Florida
Fort Clatsop	Oregon
General Grant	New York
Johnstown Flood	Pennsylvania
Korean War Veterans	Washington, D.C.
Lincoln Boyhood	Indiana
Lincoln Memorial	Washington, D.C.
Lyndon B. Johnson Grove	Washington, D.C.
Mount Rushmore	South Dakota
Oklahoma City Memorial	Oklahoma
Theodore Roosevelt Island	Washington, D.C.
Thomas Jefferson Memorial	Washington, D.C.
USS ARIZONA	Hawaii
Vietnam Veterans Memorial	Washington, D.C.
Washington Monument	Washington, D.C.
Wright Brothers	North Carolina

WHITE HOUSE — Washington, D.C.

NATIONAL MALL — Washington, D.C.

NATIONAL BATTLEFIELDS, PARKS, & SITES — *Location*

Antietam	Maryland
Big Hole	Montana
Brices Cross Roads	Mississippi
Cowpens	South Carolina
Fort Donelson	Tennessee
Fort Necessity	Pennsylvania Mountain
Manassas	Virginia
Richmond	Virginia
Monocacy	Maryland
Moores Creek	North Carolina
Petersburg	Virginia
Stones River	Tennessee
Tupelo	Mississippi
Wilson's Creek	Missouri

NATIONAL MILITARY PARKS — *Location*

Chickamauga and Chattanooga	Georgia/Tennessee
Fort Donelson	Tennessee
Fredericksburg and Spotsylvania County	Virginia
Gettysburg	Pennsylvania
Guilford Court House	North Carolina
Horseshoe Bend	Alabama
Kings Mountain	South Carolina
Pea Ridge	Arkansas
Shiloh	Tennessee
Vicksburg	Mississippi

NATIONAL SCENIC TRAILS — *Location*

Appalachian	Maine to Georgia
Natchez Trace	Alabama-Mississippi-Tennessee
Potomac Heritage	Maryland-Washington, D.C.-Virginia-Pennsylvania

NATIONAL MONUMENTS	Location
Booker T. Washington	Virginia
Cabrillo	California
Cape Krusenstern	Alaska
Castillo de SanMarco	Florida
Castle Clinton	New York
Cedar Breaks	Utah
Craters of the Moon	Idaho
Custer Battlefield	Montana
Death Valley	California/Nevada
Devils Tower	Wyoming
Fort McHenry	Maryland
Fort Sumter	South Carolina
Fort Union	New Mexico
Gila Cliff Dwellings	New Mexico
Lava Beds	California
Montezuma Castle	Arizona
Muir Woods	California
Natural Bridges	Utah
Oregon Caves	Oregon
Pipestone	Minnesota
Rainbow Bridge	Utah
Saguaro	Arizona
Scott's Bluff	Nebraska
Statue of Liberty	New Jersey/New York
White Sands	New Mexico

NATIONAL HISTORIC SITES	Location
Andersonville	Georgia
Carl Sandburg Home	North Carolina
Home of Franklin and Eleanor Roosevelt	New York
Ford's Theatre	Washington, D.C.
Fort Laramie	Wyoming
Golden Spike	Utah
Lincoln Home	Springfield, Illinois
Birthplace of Martin Luther King, Jr.	Atlanta, Georgia
Birthplace of Theodore Roosevelt	New York, New York
Pennsylvania Avenue	Washington, D.C.
Tuskegee Institute	Alabama

NATIONAL PRESERVES	Location
Aniakchak	Alaska
Bering Land Bridge	Alaska
Big Cypress	Florida
Big Thicket	Texas
Denati	Alaska
Gates of the Arctic	Alaska
Glacier Bay	Alaska
Katmai	Alaska
Lake Clark	Alaska
Noatak	Alaska
Wrangell-St. Elias	Alaska

WHATCHAMACALLITS & DOOHICKEYS

INVENTION/DISCOVERY	DATE	INVENTOR
Adding machine	1885	Burroughs
Addressograph	1892	Duncan
Aerosol spray	1941	Goodhue
Air brake	1868	Westinghouse
Air conditioning	1911	Carrier
Airplane, automatic pilot	1929	Green
Airplane, experimental	1896	Langley
Airplane with motor	1903	Wright brothers
Airplane, hydro	1911	Curtiss
Automobile, electric	1892	Morrison
Automobile, gasoline	1892	Duryea
Automobile self-starter	1911	Kettering
Automobile, steam	1889	Roper
Bifocal lens	1780	Franklin
Bomb, depth	1916	Tait
Camera, Kodak	1888	Eastman and Walker
Camera, Polaroid Land	1948	Land
Carding machine	1797	Whitemore
Carpet sweeper	1876	Bissell
Cash register	1879	Ritty
Computer, automatic sequence	1939	Aiken, et.al.
Condenser microphone (telephone)	1920	Wente
Corn, hybrid	1917	Jones
Cotton gin	1793	Whitney
Electric fan	1882	Wheeler
Elevator brake	1852	Otis
Elevator, push button	1922	Larson
Engine, gas, compound	1926	Eickemeyer
Engine, gasoline	1872	Brayton, G.
Engraving, half-tone	1893	Ives
Filament, tungsten	1915	Langmuir
Flatiron, electric	1882	Seeley
Gasoline, lead ethyl	1922	Midgley
Gyrocompass	1911	Sperry
Harvester-thresher	1888	Matteson
Helicopter	1939	Sikorsky
Ice-making machine	1851	Gorrie
Iron lung	1928	Drinker & Slaw
Lamp, arc	1879	Brush
Lamp, incandescent	1879	Edison
Lamp, incandescent, frosted	1924	Pipkin
Lamp, incandescent, gas	1916	Langmuir
Lamp, Klieg	1911	Kliegl, A. & J.
Lamp, mercury vapor	1912	Hewitt
Lathe, turret	1845	Fitch
Lens, fused bifocal	1908	Borsch

INVENTION/DISCOVERY	DATE	INVENTOR
Lightning rod	1752	Franklin
Linotype	1885	Mergenthaler
Lock, cylinder	1865	Yale
Locomotive, electric	1851	Vail
Locomotive, first U.S.	1830	Cooper, P.
Loudspeaker, dynamic	1924	Rice & Kellogg
Machine gun	1861	Gatling
Magnet, electro	1828	Henry
Mason jar	1858	Mason
Meter, induction	1888	Shallenberger
Microphone	1877	Berliner
Monotype	1887	Lanston
Motor, AC	1892	Tesla
Motor, induction	1887	Tesla
Movie machine	1894	Jenkins
Movie, panoramic	1952	Waller
Movie, talking	1927	Warner Bros.
Mower, lawn	1868	Hills
Mowing machine	1831	Manning
Nylon synthetic	1930	Carothers
Nylon	1937	DuPont lab.
Paper machine	1809	Dickinson
Pen, ballpoint	1888	Loud
Pen, fountain	1884	Waterman
Phonograph	1877	Edison
Photo, color	1892	Ives
Photo film, celluloid	1887	Goodwin
Photo film, transparent	1878	Eastman & Goodwin
Photographic paper	1898	Baekeland
Pin, safety	1849	Hunt
Plow, cast iron	1797	Newbold
Plow, disc	1896	Hardy
Pneumatic hammer	1890	King
Printing press, rotary	1846	Hoe
Printing press, web	1865	Bullock
Propeller, screw	1804	Stevens
Radar	1922	Taylor & Young
Radio amplifier	1907	DeForest
Radio beacon	1928	Donovan
Radio crystal oscillator	1918	Nicolson
Radio receiver, cascade tuning	1913	Alexanderson
Radio receiver, heterodyne	1913	DeForest
Radio, FM 2-path	1929	Armstrong
Razor, electric	1931	Schick
Razor, safety	1895	Gillette
Reaper	1834	McCormick
Record, cylinder	1887	Bell & Tainter
Record, disc	1887	Berliner

INVENTION/DISCOVERY	DATE	INVENTOR
Record, long-playing	1948	Goldmark
Record, wax cylinder	1888	Edison
Refrigerator car	1868	David
Rocket engine	1929	Goddard
Rubber, vulcanized	1839	Goodyear
Searchlight, arc	1915	Sperry
Sewing machine	1846	Howe
Shoe-sewing machine	1860	McKay
Sleeping car	1858	Pullman
Steamboat, practical	1807	Fulton
Steel alloy	1891	Harvey
Steel alloy, high speed	1901	Taylor & White
Stethoscope, binaural	1840	Cammann
Stock ticker	1870	Edison
Stove, electric	1896	Hadaway
Submarine	1891	Holland
Submarine, torpedo	1776	Bushnell
Telegraph, magnetic	1837	Morse
Telegraph, railroad	1887	Woods
Telephone amplifier	1912	DeForest
Telephone, automatic	1891	Stowger
Telephone, radio	1902	Poulsen & Fessenden
Telephone, radio	1906	DeForest
Telephone, radio, l.d.	1915	AT&T
Telephone, wireless	1899	Collins
Teletype	1928	Morkrum & Kleinschmidt
Television, iconoscope	1923	Zworykin
Television, electronic	1927	Farnsworth
Time recorder	1890	Bundy
Toaster, automatic	1918	Strite
Torpedo, marine	1804	Fulton
Tractor, crawler	1900	Holt
Transformer, Alternating Current	1885	Stanley
Transistor	1947	Shockley, Brattain & Bardeen
Trolley car, electric	1887	Van DePoele & Sprague
Turbine, gas	1899	Curtis, C. G.
Turbine, hydraulic	1849	Francis
Turbine, steam	1896	Curtis, C. G.
Typewriter	1868	Soule & Glidden
Vacuum cleaner, electric	1907	Spangler
Washer, electric	1907	Hurley Co.
Welding, atomic hydrogen	1924	Langmuir & Palmer
Welding, electric	1877	Thomson
Wind tunnel	1923	Munk
Wire, barbed	1875	Haisn
X-ray tube	1913	Coolidge
Zipper	1891	Judson

OUR PRIDE & JOY

PROMINENT AMERICAN WOMEN

Addams, Jane

Albright, Madeleine

Alcott, Louisa May

Anthony, Susan B.

Barton, Clara

Bethune, Mary McLeod

Blackwell, Elizabeth

Buck, Pearl S.

Cassatt, Mary

Chisholm, Shirley

Dickinson, Emily

Dix, Dorothea

Eddy, Mary Baker

Ederle, Gertrude

Ferraro, Geraldine

Ginsberg, Ruth Bader

Howe, Julia Ward

Jordan, Barbara

Mead, Margaret

Mott, Lucretia

O'Connor, Sandra Day

Pocahontas

Reno, Janet

Roosevelt, Eleanor

Stanton, Elizabeth Cady

Stone, Lucy

Stowe, Harriet Beecher

Truth, Sojourner

Tubman, Harriet

Warren, Mercy Otis

Wheatley, Phillis

ARTISTS/SCULPTORS

Audubon, John James

Benton, Thomas Hart

Bingham, George Caleb

Borglum, Gutzon

Cassatt, Mary

Catlin, George

Currier, Nathaniel

Homer, Winslow

Leutze, Emanuel

Moses, Grandma

O'Keefe, Georgia

Peale, Charles Wilson

Remington, Frederic

Rockwell, Norman

Ryder, Albert Pinkham

Saint-Gaudens, Augustus

Sargent, John Singer

Stuart, Gilbert

Trumbull, John

Warhol, Andy

Whistler, James Abbott McNeill

Willard, Archibald M.

Wood, Grant

NATIVE AMERICANS

Black Hawk

Chief Joseph

Cochise

Crazy Horse

Geronimo

Hiawatha

Massassoit

Osceola

Pocahontas

Pontiac

Powhatan

Red Cloud

Sacagawea

Sitting Bull

Tecumseh

U.S. Social Studies Yellow Pages, Rev. Ed.

BLACK AMERICANS

Aaron, Henry "Hank"

Abernathy, Ralph

Armstrong, Louis

Baldwin, James

Banneker, Benjamin

Basie, Count

Beckworth, James P.

Bethune, Mary McLeod

Bond, Julian

Bouchet, Edward

Bradley, Thomas

Brooks, Gwendolyn

Carruthers, George E.

Carver, George Washington

Chisholm, Shirley

Douglass, Frederick

Ellington, Duke

Evers, Medgar

Henson, Mathew

Hughes, Langston

Jackson, Jesse

Jordan, Barbara

King, Martin Luther, Jr.

Malcolm X

Marshall, Thurgood

Morrison, Toni

Parks, Rosa

Powell, Colin

Robinson, Jackie

Scott, Dred

Truth, Sojourner

Tubman, Harriet

Turner, Nat

Washington, Booker T.

Wheatley, Phillis

Young, Andrew

MILITARY LEADERS

Abrams, Creighton

Allen, Ethan

Arnold, Henry "Hap"

Bradley, Omar N.

Custer, George A.

Decatur, Stephen

Dewey, George

Eisenhower, Dwight D.

Farragut, David

Grant, Ulysses S.

Halsey, William F.

Jackson, Thomas "Stonewall"

Jones, John Paul

Kearny, Stephen

Lee, Robert E.

MacArthur, Douglas

Marshall, George C.

McClellan, George

Nimitz, Chester

Patton, George

Pershing, John

Powell, Colin

Schwarzkopf, Norman

Sheridan, Phillip

Sherman, William Tecumseh

Stuart, J.E.B.

Washington, George

Westmoreland, William

MUSICIANS & COMPOSERS

Arlen, Harold

Armstrong, Louis

Bacharach, Burt

Berlin, Irving

Bernstein, Leonard

Bock, Jerry

Brown, Nacio Herb

Carmichael, Hoagy

Cohan, George M.

Copland, Aaron

Ellington, Duke

Foster, Stephen Collins

Gershwin, George

Gershwin, Ira

Hamlisch, Marvin

Hammerstein, Oscar II

Howe, Julia Ward

Joplin, Scott

Lerner, Alan J.

Loewe, Frederick

Mancini, Henry

Mercer, Johnny

Porter, Cole

Rodgers, Richard

Sousa, John Philip

POLITICAL LEADERS

Adams, Samuel

Austin, Stephen

Bradford, William

Bryan, William Jennings

Burger, Warren

Calhoun, John C.

Chase, Salmon P.

Chisholm, Shirley

Clay, Henry

Daley, Richard

Davis, Jefferson

Dewey, Thomas E.

Dirksen, Everett M.

Dole, Robert

Douglas, Stephen A.

Dulles, John Foster

Ferraro, Geraldine

Franklin, Benjamin

Goldwater, Barry

Hamilton, Alexander

Hancock, John

Henry, Patrick

Hoover, J. Edgar

Houston, Samuel

Humphrey, Hubert

Jordan, Barbara

Kennedy, Robert

Kissinger, Henry

Lodge, Henry Cabot

Paine, Thomas

Smith, John

Stevenson, Adlai

Webster, Daniel

Young, Andrew

SCIENTISTS/INVENTORS

Aiken, Howard H.

Carruthers, George E.

Carver, George
    Washington

DeForest, Lee

Eastman, George

Edison, Thomas A.

Einstein, Albert

Ford, Henry

Franklin, Benjamin

Goddard, Robert H.

Hubble, Edwin P.

Land, Edwin

Noyce, Robert N.

Reed, Walter S.

Whitney, Eli

Wright Brothers

WRITERS/AUTHORS

Alcott, Louisa May

Baldwin, James

Brooks, Gwendolyn

Buck, Pearl S.

Cooper, John Fenimore

Dickinson, Emily

Emerson, Ralph Waldo

Faulkner, William

Fitzgerald, F. Scott

Frost, Robert

Hawthorne, Nathaniel

Hemingway, Ernest

Holmes, Oliver Wendell

Hughes, Langston

Irving, Washington

Key, Francis Scott

Lewis, Sinclair

London, Jack

Longfellow, Henry Wadsworth

Melville, Herman

Morrison, Toni

Poe, Edgar Allen

Pulitzer, Joseph

Sandburg, Carl

Sinclair, Upton

Steinbeck, John

Stowe, Harriet Beecher

Thoreau, Henry David

Twain, Mark
*(actual name:
Samuel Langhorne Clemens)*

Warren, Mercy Otis

Whitman, Walt

OTHERS

Astor, John Jacob

Carnegie, Andrew

Darrow, Clarence

Disney, Walt

Firestone, Harvey

Flagler, Henry M.

Hearst, William Randolph

Hilton, Conrad

Hughes, Howard

Johnson, Howard

Kellogg, Will K.

Kroc, Ray A.

Lindbergh, Charles

Mann, Horace

Mead, Margaret

Morgan, J. Pierpont

Nader, Ralph

Paley, William S.

Penn, William

Penny, James C.

Procter, William C.

Rockefeller, John D.

Sarnoff, David

Sears, Richard W.

Strauss, Levi

Vanderbilt, Cornelius

Walgreen, Charles R.

Ward, Aaron Montgomery

Woolworth, Frank W.

Wright, Frank Lloyd

Wrigley, William, Jr.

LARGER THAN LIFE CHARACTERS

JOHNNY APPLESEED (1774–1845)

An American pioneer who planted apple seeds and sprouts throughout the frontier regions of western Pennsylvania, Ohio, Indiana, and Illinois. His real name was John Chapman. He is remembered as part planter, part preacher of the early 1800s.

SAM BASS (1851–1878)

Considered the "Robin Hood" of Texas. He was labeled a "good badman" because he led a gang of bank and train robbers to steal from the rich and give to the poor. The legend of Sam Bass continues in the form of a ballad and the many stories about his generosity.

DANIEL BOONE (1734–1820)

The most famous pioneer of colonial times. He explored Kentucky and created the Wilderness Road, a famous route followed by many pioneers as they traveled west. He was considered a natural leader and a generous man. In conflicts he avoided bloodshed as much as possible. He is known as the "ideal" frontiers-man courageous, quick-thinking, determined, and skilled.

BUFFALO BILL (1846–1917)

Earned his nickname by his skill with a rifle and the number of buffaloes he killed to supply meat for workmen building a western railroad. His real name was William Frederick Cody. He was well known as a frontiersman of the American West and later as a famous circus entertainer in "Wild West" shows.

PAUL BUNYAN

The legendary hero of lumberjacks. Paul was big, strong, and smart. He owned a giant blue ox named Babe. Many tall tales and stories were told about these two, who were able to haul logs better and faster than anyone.

KIT CARSON (1809–1868)

A famous American frontiersman. He was a trapper, a hunter, a guide, and a soldier. He was known for his perilous adventures west of the Mississippi River. His legendary exploits and travels took him from Missouri to New Mexico, into California, Wyoming, Idaho, Colorado, through the Rocky Mountains, into Oregon, and back to California. He fought the Confederate forces in the Civil War and led several campaigns against Indian tribes. He was made a brigadier general in 1865.

DAVY CROCKETT (1786–1836)

One of the most famous frontiersmen in United States history. He was a skilled hunter, soldier, scout, humorist, and a successful and popular Tennessee Congressman. Davy Crockett was killed in battle at the Alamo on March 6, 1836.

FEBOLD FEBOLDSON

A mythical, tall-tale hero of Nebraska created by two newspapermen in the mid-1920s. He was called the "Big Swede." He was humorous and clever as he solved problems and lived through hardships of that era.

U.S. Social Studies Yellow Pages, Rev. Ed.

MIKE FINK (1770–1823)

The subject of many folk tales, this American frontiersman, boatman, and trapper was famous as an expert shot as he served as an Indian scout in Pennsylvania. He is described as big, strong, and boastful.

CASEY JONES (1864–1900)

A courageous railroad engineer who saved the lives of passengers and crew when he held the air brake lever as the engine crashed into the rear of two freight trains in Mississippi. He was killed in the crash. His courage and skill are the subjects of a well-known American folk song, "Casey Jones".

JOHN HENRY

Legendary black figure in American folklore, known for his strength as a steel driver. Henry used a long-handled hammer to pound a steel drill into rock to be blasted with explosives during railroad construction in West Virginia. He symbolized manual workers' and gang labor's last stand against the machine. It is said that he died in a race with a steam drill when a blood vessel burst in his head.

PECOS BILL

A mythical super-cowboy character in American folklore. He was supposedly raised by coyotes after he fell from a wagon train. He is credited with inventing roping and other cowboy skills and is the subject of many tall tales.

POCAHONTAS (1595?–1617)

The name means "playful one." She was the daughter of an American Indian chief, Powhatan. Supposedly, at the age of twelve she saved the life of Captain John Smith when her father was about to kill him. She was held captive on a British ship in 1613, fell in love with an English settler named John Rolfe, converted to Christianity, and married Rolfe. In 1616 they went to England where she was considered an Indian "princess."

RIP VAN WINKLE

A famous character from American folklore. He was created by Washington Irving in 1819. He was happy-go-lucky and enjoyed fishing and hunting much more than being at home or at work. In one of the stories, he falls asleep for twenty years. When he awakens he is recognized by his children and accepted into his village.

SACAGAWEA (1787?–1812?)

The interpreter and principal guide for the Lewis and Clark Expedition to the Pacific Ocean in 1804–1805. She was born into the Shoshoni Indian tribe of Idaho but was taken by an enemy tribe and sold as a slave. Because of her Shoshoni relatives, she was able to help the Lewis and Clark expedition. Her name means "Bird Woman." Many theories are suggested but no facts are known about her death.

ALFRED BULLTOP STORMALONG

An American folklore character who was a legendary hero of sailors. He sailed on the Courser, a huge ship, on which he was an amazing seaman. One story tells that he suggested soaping the sides of the ship to allow it to pass through the English Channel— such a tight squeeze that the soap rubbed off, leaving the cliffs of Dover white!

HAIL TO THE CHIEF!

Number	President	Party	Vice President	Term
1	George Washington	None	John Adams	1789–1797
2	John Adams	Federalist	Thomas Jefferson	1797–1801
3	Thomas Jefferson	Dem.-Rep.	Aaron Burr, George Clinton	1801–1809
4	James Madison	Dem.-Rep.	George Clinton, Elbridge Gerry	1809–1817
5	James Monroe	Dem.-Rep.	Daniel D. Tompkins	1817–1825
6	John Quincy Adams	Dem.-Rep.	John C. Calhoun	1825–1829
7	Andrew Jackson	Democrat	John C. Calhoun, Martin Van Buren	1829–1837
8	Martin Van Buren	Democrat	Richard M. Johnson	1837–1841
9	William Henry Harrison	Whig	John Tyler	1841
10	John Tyler	Whig	—	1841–1845
11	James K. Polk	Democrat	George M. Dallas	1845–1849
12	Zachary Taylor	Whig	Millard Fillmore	1849–1850
13	Millard Fillmore	Whig	—	1850–1853
14	Franklin Pierce	Democrat	William R. King	1853–1857
15	James Buchanan	Democrat	John C. Breckenridge	1857–1861
16	Abraham Lincoln	Republican	Hannibal Hamlin, Andrew Johnson	1861–1865
17	Andrew Johnson	Democrat	—	1865–1869
18	Ulysses S. Grant	Republican	Schuyler Colfax	1869–1877
19	Rutherford B. Hayes	Republican	William A. Wheeler	1877–1881
20	James A. Garfield	Republican	Chester A. Arthur	1881
21	Chester A. Arthur	Republican	—	1881–1885

U.S. Social Studies Yellow Pages, Rev. Ed.

Number	President	Party	Vice President	Term
22	Grover Cleveland	Democrat	Thomas A. Hendricks	1885–1889
23	Benjamin Harrison	Republican	Levi P. Morton	1889–1893
24	Grover Cleveland	Democrat	Adlai E. Stevenson	1893–1897
25	William McKinley	Republican	Garret A. Hobart	1897–1901
26	Theodore Roosevelt	Republican	Charles W. Fairbanks	1901–1909
27	William H. Taft	Republican	James S. Sherman	1909–1913
28	Woodrow Wilson	Democrat	Thomas R. Marshall	1913–1921
29	Warren G. Harding	Republican	Calvin Coolidge	1921–1923
30	Calvin Coolidge	Republican	Charles G. Dawes	1923–1929
31	Herbert C. Hoover	Republican	Charles Curtis	1929–1933
32	Franklin D. Roosevelt	Democrat	John Nance Garner, Henry A. Wallace, Harry S. Truman	1933–1945
33	Harry S. Truman	Democrat	Alben W. Barkley	1945–1953
34	Dwight D. Eisenhower	Republican	Richard M. Nixon	1953–1961
35	John F. Kennedy	Democrat	Lyndon B. Johnson	1961–1963
36	Lyndon B. Johnson	Democrat	Hubert Humphrey	1963–1969
37	Richard M. Nixon	Republican	Spiro T. Agnew	1969–1974
38	Gerald R. Ford	Republican	Nelson A. Rockefeller	1974–1977
39	Jimmy Carter	Democrat	Walter Mondale	1977–1981
40	Ronald Reagan	Republican	George Bush	1981–1989
41	George Bush	Republican	J. Danforth Quayle	1989–1992
42	Bill Clinton	Democrat	Albert Gore, Jr.	1992–2001
43	George W. Bush	Republican	Richard B. Cheney	2001–

HISTORY & GOVERNMENT ABCs

abolitionist — person who wanted to end slavery

ally — a friend in a war

amendment — an addition to the constitution

armistice — a written agreement to stop fighting

balance of power — equal military and economic strength between two or more nations

Bill of Rights — the first ten amendments to the Constitution

bureaucracy — a body of government officials and employees

cabinet — people chosen by the President to be advisers and to head executive departments

capitalism — economic system of the U.S.; individuals control production of goods and services and government intervention is limited

carpetbagger — a Northerner who went to the South after the Civil War to profit financially

cash crop — a crop grown to sell and make a profit

century — a period of one hundred years

checks and balances — a system in which each branch of the government has controls over the power of the other branches

civil rights — the rights of citizens to receive equal treatment, both in law and in practice

colonist — a person who leaves a mother country to live in a colony

Congress — the legislative branch of the U.S. government made up of the Senate and the House of Representatives

compromise — to give up some of what one wants in order to reach an agreement

containment — U.S. policy during the 1950s and 1960s aimed at limiting the spread of communism

culture — the way of life shared by a group of people

decade — a period of ten years

declaration — a formal statement

delegate — a person elected by people to represent them

demilitarized zone — a zone or strip of land not controlled or used only by the military

democracy — rule by the people

depression — a period of steep economic decline

disarmament — reduction or limitation in the number of weapons

Domino Theory — key idea of U.S. foreign policy in the 1950s–1970s: belief that if a country fell to communism, the countries around it would also fall

economy — the way people use resources to produce and sell goods and services

U.S. Social Studies Yellow Pages, Rev. Ed.

elector — a person selected in a state to cast an electoral vote for president

executive — the management branch of the government

federal — a form of government in which powers are shared between the states and the national government

free enterprise — the economic system in which there is little government control over business practices

frontier — the area that separates settled land and the wilderness

heritage — a common way of thinking, believing, and doing things passed down from preceding generations

historian — a person who studies the past

homesteader — a person who was given 160 acres of land by the government after living on it for five years

House of Representatives — one of the houses of the U.S. Congress

immigrant — a person who leaves one country to live in another country

impeachment — formal charge of wrongdoing brought against an elected official of the federal government

imperialism — the practices of establishing and controlling colonies

inauguration — the ceremony in which the President takes the oath of office

independence — freedom from control by others

inflation — the rise in prices

isolationism — a national policy of maintaining a nation's interests without being involved with other countries

judicial — the branch of government that is the court system

legislative — the lawmaking branch of government

legislature — a state lawmaking body

liberty — freedom

melting pot — the idea that immigrants of various cultural backgrounds gradually adapt to American ways

nationalism — patriotic feelings for one's country

neutrality — the policy of avoiding ties with other nations or deep involvement in wars or other affairs

official — a person either elected or appointed to do a community or government job

patriot — a person who believed that the American colonists had the right to stand up for their liberties

pilgrim — a person from England who settled at Plymouth

pioneer — one of the first people to settle or enter a new territory

president — the head of the executive, or management, branch of government

popular vote — a vote of the people

propaganda — ideas spread in order to gain public support for a cause or to damage an opposing cause

radical — person who favors extreme or sudden changes

ratify — to approve by voting

recall — process of removing an elected official from office by public vote

referendum — a legal process by which people can revoke a law passed by the legislature

regulatory — government group that supervises a business operation

reparations — money given by defeated nations as payment for damages suffered by other nations during a war

repeal — to repeal or reject a law

republic — a form of government in which people elect representatives

revolution — a major, sudden change in government and people's lives

scalawag — a Southern white in the Republican party during Reconstruction

secession — withdrawal from a group, nation, or association

segregation — the practice of separating people on the basis of racial religious, or social difference

separatist — a person who withdrew or separated from the Church of England (Pilgrim)

Senate — one of the legislative bodies of the U.S. Congress

society — a broad grouping of people who are bound by common laws, traditions, and activities

states rights — the doctrine that holds that the states have powers that are not assigned to the federal government by the Constitution

strike — refusal of workers to work until demand for better wages or working conditions are met

suffrage — the right to vote

summit meeting — a meeting held between the heads of two countries to settle political issues

Supreme Court — the court within the judicial branch of the government that has the power to decide whether laws are constitutional

temperance — the movement to restrict the drinking of alcoholic beverages

third party — a political group organized to compete against the two major political parties

territory — an area of land belonging to a government

treaty — a formal agreement to maintain peace

two-party system — a political system with two major parties of similar strength

tyranny — harsh and unjust rule

unconstitutional — not in keeping with or supported by the Constitution's laws

veto — to refuse to sign a proposed law

xenophobia — the fear of foreigners or strangers

U. S. GEOGRAPHY
GEOGRAPHICAL PORTRAITS

APPALACHIAN HIGHLANDS

This region extends from the top of main along the Pacific Coast south to Alabama. It is east of the Continental Interior Plain that extends from northern Maine to Alabama.

Characterized by:
worn down peaks
beautiful lakes
thin rocky soil
40–60 inches annual
   rainfall

Features:
White Mountains
Green Mountains
Allegheny Mountains
Adirondack Mountains
Catskill Mountains
Blue Ridge Mountains
Great Smoky Mountains
Hudson Highland
Appalachian Plateau
Finger Lakes
Connecticut River
Potomac River
Susquehanna River
Delaware River
Hudson River

Products:
coal, iron ore, oil
hydroelectric power
center of trade, commerce,
industry
fishing industry

Great Valleys:
East Tennessee Valley
Shenandoah Valley
Rome Valley
Great Valley of Alabama
Lehigh Valley
Lebanon Valley
Cumberland Valley
Shenandoah Valley

COASTAL PLAINS

This region extends across the eastern and southern part of the country as far west as eastern Texas.

Characterized by:
rolling plains
swamps
dairy farms
orchards
numerous rivers
river rapids
long beaches
many offshore islands
natural harbors
bays
waterfalls
forests

Features:
Gulf Coastal Plain
Atlantic Coastal Plain
The Piedmont
Susquehanna River
Hudson River
Potomac River
Delaware River
Savannah River
Long Island Sound
Chesapeake Bay
Delaware Bay

Products:
manufacturing
shipping
tourism
tobacco
fruit, vegetables
fishing

OZARK-OUACHITA HIGHLANDS

These lie between the coastal lowland plains and the interior Plains, stretching from southeastern Missouri west to eastern Oklahoma.

Characterized by:
high plains
deep gorges
streams and rivers
underground caves
fertile river valleys
poor soil in highlands
rugged terrain

Features:
Ouachita Mountains

Products:
dairy products
petroleum
natural gas
springs
forests
hills
minerals
coal, iron ore

CONTINENTAL INTERIOR PLAINS

These cover the area between the Appalachian Highlands and the Rocky Mountains.

Characterized by:
broad plains
rich soil
forests in the east
few trees in west
hills in the north

flat land
farming
Features:
the Great Lakes
Mississippi River
Ohio River

Products:
corn and wheat
metal ores
petroleum

ROCKY MOUNTAINS

These stretch from Alaska to northern New Mexico.

Characterized by:
high peaks
forests on lower slopes
rivers
rich in metals & minerals
ranching
grazing
tourism, beauty

large wild animals
lumbering
Features:
Great Divide
Colorado River
Missouri River
Rio Grande River

Products:
metals
beef
dairy products
oil & natural gas
timber

WESTERN RANGES, BASINS, & PLATEAUS

These lie west of the Rocky Mountains in a region that stretches from Washington south to Mexico.

Characterized by:
dry weather
deserts
open ranch land
irrigation
interesting landforms

rivers & river gorges
plateaus
livestock
Features:
Grand Canyon
Colorado River

Columbia Plateau
Great Salt Lake
Great Basin
Death Valley
Great Salt Lake Desert

PACIFIC RANGES & LOWLANDS

This area reaches all along the Pacific Ocean, from Washington south through California, west from the Cascade Mountains.

Characterized by:
high mountains
forests
waterfalls
lakes
volcanic activity
fertile valleys
bays
beaches

vineyards
harbors
Features:
Cascade Mountains
Sierra Nevada Mountains
Mt. St. Helen
San Francisco Bay
Puget Sound
Columbia River

San Diego Bay
Products:
wine grapes
fruits
vegetables
timber
fishing
tourism

U.S. Social Studies Yellow Pages, Rev. Ed.

FROM SEA TO SHINING SEA

The continental U.S. is generally divided into seven regions, each with a particular cultural and geographic uniqueness.

The New England States

A small region in the northeast corner of the country, known for its beautiful autumn colors and rural landscape, this is the home of many historic sites. Its land is too rocky and hilly for much agriculture, but it produces many dairy and poultry products. It is home to the Green Mountains, the Connecticut River, and Boston, its largest city.

Maine	Massachusetts
Connecticut	New Hampshire
Vermont	Rhode Island

The Mid-Atlantic States

This region is the most densely populated in the country, making a home for several large cities such as New York, Newark, Pittsburgh, Buffalo, and Philadelphia. Its many harbors make it a worldwide trade center. There is coal mining in the Appalachian Mountain region. These mountains also attract hikers and vacationers. The region is filled with farms, lakes, and sandy beaches along its Atlantic coast and many lakes.

New Jersey	New York
Pennsylvania	

The Southern States

This region has been a major agricultural area for the country. The tourist business is also healthy because of the beautiful mountains and the Atlantic and Gulf beaches. Miami, New Orleans, Baltimore, Memphis, and Washington D. C. are some of the major cities in the region.

Delaware	Maryland
West Virginia	Virginia
North Carolina	South Carolina
Louisiana	Kentucky
Tennessee	Georgia
Alabama	Mississippi
Arkansas	Florida

The Midwestern States

This region is primarily a plains region, covering much of the central part of the country. With its rich soil, this is a main region for producing wheat, corn, and livestock. It is home to Chicago, Milwaukee, Detroit, and the Mississippi River.

Ohio	Michigan
Missouri	Kansas
Wisconsin	Indiana
Illinois	Nebraska
Iowa	Minnesota
North Dakota	South Dakota

The Rocky Mountain States

The centerpiece of this region is the Rocky Mountains. The region also has plains, plateaus, forests, and deserts. It is a rich ranching and mining area. Its beauty attracts many tourists. It is the home to the Colorado River and the city of Denver.

Colorado	Wyoming
Nevada	Utah
Montana	Idaho

The Southwestern States

This is a region of large cattle ranches and fields of crops such as cotton. The region was made especially wealthy by the oil and natural gas beneath its surface. It is also a region of pleasant, dry weather that attracts tourists and permanent residents alike. It is the home to the Grand Canyon and other areas of great beauty. Its largest cities are Dallas, Houston, and Phoenix.

Arizona	Texas
New Mexico	Oklahoma

The Pacific Coast States

This region borders the Pacific Ocean. It has a long, beautiful coastline, forests and mountains. The coasts supply fish; the forests supply timber, and the valleys produce vegetables, fruits, and wine. It is a region of manufacturing and technology. The largest city is Los Angeles.

Oregon	California
Washington	

WATER, WATER EVERYWHERE!

MAJOR U.S. RIVERS

Name	Length (miles)
Arkansas	1,459
Colorado (Arizona)	1,450
Columbia	1,243
Mississippi	2,340
Mississippi, Upper	1,171
Mississippi-Missouri-Red Rock	3,710
Missouri	2,315
Missouri-Red Rock	2,540
Ohio	981
Ohio-Allegheny	1,306
Peace	1,210
Red (Oklahoma, Texas, Louisiana)	1,290
Rio Grande	1,900
Snake	1,038
Yukon	1,979

MAJOR U.S. LAKES

Canandaigua Lake
Crater Lake
Finger Lakes
Great Lakes
    Lake Erie
    Lake Huron
    Lake Michigan
    Lake Ontario
    Lake Superior
Great Salt Lake
Guntersville Lake
Kentucky Lake
Lake Champlain
Lake Cumberland
Lake George
Lake Mead
Lake Memphremagog
Lake of the Ozarks
Lake of the Woods
Lake Okeechobee

Lake O' the Cherokees
Lake Ouachita
Lake Placid
Lake Pontchartrain
Lake Powell
Lake Saint Clair
Lake Saint Lawrence
Lake Tahoe
Lake Texoma
Lake Winnebago
Lake Winnipesaukee
Oneida Lake
Pend Orielle Lake
Rainy Lake
Reelfoot Lake
Salton Sea
Saranac Lakes
Utah Lake

U.S. Social Studies Yellow Pages, Rev. Ed.

MAJOR U.S. WATERFALLS

Name	Location	Elevation (feet)
Yosemite Falls	Yosemite National Park, California	2,425
Ribbon Falls	Yosemite National Park, California	1,612
Silver Strand Falls	Yosemite, California	1,170
Feather Falls	Fall River, California	640
Bridalveil Falls	Yosemite National Park, California	620
Multnomah Falls	Oregon	620
Nevada Falls	Merced River, Yosemite, California	594
Akaka Falls	Kolekole Str., Hawaii	442
Illilouette	Yosemite National Park, California	370
Vernal Falls	Merced River, Yosemite, California	317
Seven Falls	South Cheyenne Cr., Colorado	300
Lower Yellowstone Falls	Wyoming	308
Sluiskin Falls	Paradise River, Washington	300
Snoqualmie Falls	Washington	268
Fall Creek Falls	Tennessee	256
Taughannock Falls	New York	215
Shoshone Falls	Snake River, Idaho	212
Niagara Falls	New York	176
Big Manitou Falls	Black River, Wisconsin	165
Yellowstone National Park Tower	Wyoming	132
Upper Yellowstone Falls	Wyoming	109
Great Falls	Potomac River, Maryland	71
Passaic Falls	New Jersey	70
Cumberland Falls	Kentucky	68
Minnehaha Falls	Minnesota	53

OUR TREASURE CHEST

National Park	Location
Acadia	Maine
American Samoa	Am. Samoa
Arches	Utah
Badlands	South Dakota
Big Bend	Texas
Biscayne	Florida
Bryce Canyon	Utah
Canyonlands	Utah
Capitol Reef	Utah
Carlsbad Caverns	New Mexico
Channel Islands	California
Crater Lake	Oregon
Death Valley	California
Denali	Alaska
Dry Tortugas	Florida
Everglades	Florida
Gates of the Arctic	Alaska
Glacier	Montana
Glacier Bay	Alaska
Grand Canyon	Arizona
Grand Teton	Wyoming
Great Basin	Nevada
Great Smoky Mountains	North Carolina-Tennessee
Guadalupe Mountains	Texas
Haleakala	Hawaii
Hawaii Volcanoes	Hawaii

National Park	Location
Isle Royal	Michigan
Joshua Tree	California
Katmai	Alaska
Kenai Fjords	Alaska
Kings Canyon	California
Kobuk Valley	Alaska
Lake Clark	Alaska
Lassen Volcanic	California
Mammoth Cave	Kentucky
Mesa Verde	Colorado
Mount Rainier	Washington
North Cascades	Washington
Olympic	Washington
Petrified Forest	Arizona
Redwood	California
Rocky Mountain	Colorado
Sequoia	California
Shenandoah	Virginia
Theodore Roosevelt	North Dakota
Virgin Islands	Virgin Islands
Voyageurs	Minnesota
Wind Cave	South Dakota
Wrangell-St. Elias	Alaska
Yellowstone	Idaho-Montana-Wyoming
Yosemite	California
Zion	Utah

U.S. Social Studies Yellow Pages, Rev. Ed.

STATES' STATS

STATE	Nickname	Capital	Date Admitted to Union	Population (2000)
ALABAMA	Yellowhammer State	Montgomery	1819	4,447,100
ALASKA	The Last Frontier	Juneau	1959	626,932
ARIZONA	Grand Canyon State	Phoenix	1912	5,130,632
ARKANSAS	Land of Opportunity	Little Rock	1836	2,673,400
CALIFORNIA	Golden State	Sacramento	1850	33,871,648
COLORADO	Centennial State	Denver	1876	4,301,261
CONNECTICUT	Constitution State	Hartford	1788	3,405,565
DELAWARE	Diamond State	Dover	1787	783,600
FLORIDA	Sunshine State	Tallahassee	1845	15,982,378
GEORGIA	Peach State	Atlanta	1788	8,186,453
HAWAII	Aloha State	Honolulu	1959	1,211,537
IDAHO	Gem State	Boise	1890	1,293,953
ILLINOIS	Prairie State	Springfield	1818	12,419,293
INDIANA	Hoosier State	Indianapolis	1816	6,080,485
IOWA	Hawkeye State	Des Moines	1846	2,926,324
KANSAS	Sunflower State	Topeka	1861	2,688,418
KENTUCKY	Bluegrass State	Frankfort	1792	4,041,769
LOUISIANA	Pelican State	Baton Rouge	1812	4,468,976
MAINE	Pine Tree State	Augusta	1820	1,274,923
MARYLAND	Free State	Annapolis	1788	5,296,846
MASSACHUSETTS	Bay State	Boston	1788	6,349,097
MICHIGAN	Wolverine State	Lansing	1837	9,938,444
MINNESOTA	North Star State	St. Paul	1858	4,919,479
MISSISSIPPI	Magnolia State	Jackson	1817	2,844,658
MISSOURI	Show Me State	Jefferson City	1821	5,595,211

STATE	Nickname	Capital	Date Admitted to Union	Population (2000)
MONTANA	Treasure State	Helena	1889	902,195
NEBRASKA	Cornhusker State	Lincoln	1867	1,711,263
NEVADA	Silver State	Carson City	1864	1,998,257
NEW HAMPSHIRE	Granite State	Concord	1788	1,235,786
NEW JERSEY	Garden State	Trenton	1787	8,414,350
NEW MEXICO	Land of Enchantment	Santa Fe	1912	1,819,046
NEW YORK	Empire State	Albany	1788	18,976,457
NORTH CAROLINA	Tar Heel State	Raleigh	1789	8,049,313
NORTH DAKOTA	Sioux State	Bismarck	1889	642,200
OHIO	Buckeye State	Columbus	1803	11,353,140
OKLAHOMA	Sooner State	Oklahoma City	1907	3,450,654
OREGON	Beaver State	Salem	1859	3,421,399
PENNSYLVANIA	Keystone State	Harrisburg	1787	12,281,054
RHODE ISLAND	Ocean State	Providence	1790	1,048,391
SOUTH CAROLINA	Palmetto State	Columbia	1788	4,012,012
SOUTH DAKOTA	Sunshine State	Pierre	889	754,844
TENNESSEE	Volunteer State	Nashville	1796	5,689,283
TEXAS	Lone Star State	Austin	1845	20,851,820
UTAH	Beehive State	Salt Lake City	1896	2,233,169
VERMONT	Green Mountain State	Montpelier	1791	608,827
VIRGINIA	The Old Dominion	Richmond	1788	7,078,515
WASHINGTON	Evergreen State	Olympia	1889	5,984,121
WEST VIRGINIA	Mountain State	Charleston	1863	1,808,344
WISCONSIN	Badger State	Madison	1848	5,363,675
WYOMING	Equality State	Cheyenne	1890	493,782
WASHINGTON, D.C.				572,059

WHAT'S IN A NAME?

STATE NAME	Origin of the Name
ALABAMA	From a tribe of the Creek confederacy
ALASKA	Russian version of Aleut word meaning "great land"
ARIZONA	Spanish version of Pima word meaning "little spring place"
ARKANSAS	French version of "Kansas," a Sioux word meaning "south wind people"
CALIFORNIA	Mythical island paradise in Spanish literature
COLORADO	Spanish word for "red"
CONNECTICUT	Algonquin word meaning "beside the long river"
DELAWARE	Honors Lord De La Warr, an early governor of Virginia
WASHINGTON D.C.	Honors Columbus
FLORIDA	Spanish word meaning "feast of flowers"
GEORGIA	Honors King George II
HAWAII	Polynesian word for "homeland"
IDAHO	Shoshone word for "salmon tribe" or "light on the mountains"
ILLINOIS	Algonquin word meaning "men" or "warriors"
INDIANA	Land of the Indians
IOWA	Sioux word meaning "beautiful land"
KANSAS	Sioux word meaning "south wind people"
KENTUCKY	Iroquois word meaning "meadowland"
LOUISIANA	Honors Louis XIV of France
MAINE	From "The Main," distinguished the mainland from the offshore islands
MARYLAND	Honors Queen Henrietta Marie
MASSACHUSETTS	Algonquin word for "large mountain place"
MICHIGAN	Chippewa word for "great water"
MINNESOTA	Sioux word for "sky-tinted water"
MISSISSIPPI	Chippewa word for "great river"

STATE NAME	Origin of the Name
MISSOURI	Named after tribe of Missouri Indians; means "town of large canoes"
MONTANA	Spanish word meaning "mountainous"
NEBRASKA	Omaha name for Platte River, "broad river"
NEVADA	Spanish word meaning "snow-clad"
NEW HAMPSHIRE	Named for English county of Hampshire
NEW JERSEY	Named for island of Jersey in English Channel
NEW MEXICO	Named for Aztec war god "Mexitil"
NEW YORK	Honors English Duke of York
NORTH CAROLINA	Honors King Charles I
NORTH DAKOTA	Sioux word meaning "friend" or "ally"
OHIO	Iroquois word for "beautiful river"
OKLAHOMA	Choctaw word meaning "red people"
OREGON	Native American word meaning "beautiful water"
PENNSYLVANIA	Honors Admiral William Penn, father of the founder of the colony
RHODE ISLAND	Named for Greek island of Rhodes
SOUTH CAROLINA	Honors King Charles I
SOUTH DAKOTA	Sioux word meaning "friend" or "ally"
TENNESSEE	Name of Cherokee villages on the Little Tennessee River
TEXAS	Caddo word for "friendly tribe"
UTAH	Refers to the Ute tribe, meaning "people of the mountains"
VERMONT	From the French words for "green mountain"
VIRGINIA	Honors "Virgin Queen" Elizabeth I
WASHINGTON	Honors George Washington
WEST VIRGINIA	Honors "Virgin Queen" Elizabeth I
WISCONSIN	Chippewa word for "grassy place"
WYOMING	Delaware Indian word meaning "mountains and valleys alternating"

U.S. Social Studies Yellow Pages, Rev. Ed.

CITIES ON PARADE

Top 50 Cities in the U.S. by 2000 population

City	Estimated 2000 population	City	Estimated 2000 population
New York, NY	7,429,000	Portland, OR	504,000
Los Angeles, CA	6,334,000	Fort Worth, TX	503,000
Chicago, IL	2,800,000	Cleveland, OH	502,000
Houston, TX	1,846,000	Denver, CO	500,000
Philadelphia, PA	1,418,000	Oklahoma City, OK	475,000
San Diego, CA	1,239,000	Tucson, AZ	467,000
Phoenix, AZ	1,212,000	New Orleans, LA	461,000
San Antonio, TX	1,148,000	Kansas City, MO	438,000
Dallas, TX	1,077,000	Long Beach, CA	435,000
Detroit, MI	966,000	Virginia Beach, VA	434,000
San Jose, CA	868,000	Albuquerque, NM	421,000
San Francisco, CA	747,000	Las Vegas, NV	419,000
Indianapolis, IN	739,000	Sacramento, CA	407,000
Jacksonville, FL	696,000	Fresno, CA	404,000
Columbus, OH	672,000	Atlanta, GA	402,000
Baltimore, MD	633,000	Honolulu, HI	396,000
El Paso, TX	613,000	Omaha, NE	387,000
Memphis, TN	606,000	Tulsa, OK	382,000
Austin, TX	588,000	Miami, FL	370,000
Milwaukee, WI	573,000	Mesa, AZ	369,000
Boston, MA	555,000	Oakland, CA	365,000
Seattle, WA	537,000	Minneapolis, MN	354,000
Charlotte, NC	521,000	Colorado Springs, CO	351,000
Washington, DC	519,000	Pittsburgh, PA	337,000
Nashville, TN	507,000	Wichita, KA	336,000

UNITED STATES SUPERLATIVE STATISTICS

Largest state	Alaska	591,004 sq. mi.
Smallest state	Rhode Island	1,212 sq. mi.
Most populated state	California	33,871,648 (2000 census)
Least populated state	Wyoming	493,782 (2000 census)
Most densely populated state	New Jersey	1093.8 persons per sq. mi.
Least densely populated state	Alaska	1.1 persons per sq. mi.
State with longest shoreline	Alaska	33,904 mi
State with the most area of tribal land	Arizona	20,087.538 acres
State most visited by tourists	Florida	6,100,000 visitors
Northernmost city	Barrow, Alaska	71° 17' N.
Northernmost point	Point Barrow, Alaska	71° 23' N.
Southernmost city	Hilo, Hawaii	19° 43' N.
Southernmost point	Ka Lee, Hawaii	18° 55' N. (155° 41' W.)
Easternmost city	Eastport, Maine	66° 59' 02" W.
Easternmost point	W. Quoddy Head, Maine	66° 57' W.
Westernmost city	West Unalaska, Alaska	163° 32' W.
Westernmost point	Cape Wrangell, Alaska	172° 27' E.
Highest settlement	Climax, Colorado	11,560 ft.
Lowest settlement	Calipatria, California	185 ft.
Highest waterfall	Yosemite Falls, California	2,425 ft.
Longest river	Mississippi-Missouri	3,710 mi.
Highest mountain	Mt. McKinley (Denali), Alaska	20,320 ft.
Lowest point	Death Valley, California	282 ft. below sea level
Largest lake	Lake Superior	31,820 sq. mi.
Largest island	Hawaii	4037 sq. mi.
Largest island in a lake	Isle Royal (Lake Superior, Michigan)	209 sq. mi
Highest Island	Akutan, Alaska	13,698 ft.

U.S. Social Studies Yellow Pages, Rev. Ed.

Deepest lake	Crater Lake, Oregon	1,932 ft.
Coldest City	International Falls, Minnesota	average temp: 36.8° F
Hottest City	Key West, Florida	average temp: 77.8° F
Hottest recorded temperature	Death Valley, California	134° F
Coldest recorded temperature	Prospect Creek, Alaska	−80° F
Wettest spot	Mt. Waialeale, Hawaii	460 in. annually
Driest spot	Yuma, Arizona	3.17 in. annually
Largest Native American Reservation	Navajo *(Utah-Arizona-New Mexico)*	pop: 143,500
Largest gorge	Grand Canyon, Arizona	277 mi. long, 600 ft. deep
Deepest gorge	Hell's Canyon *(Snake River, Idaho-Oregon)*	7,900 ft.
Longest Cave	Mammoth Cave System	352 mi
Tallest building	Sears Tower, Chicago, Illinois	1,454 ft. tall *(with spires: 1,707 ft.)*
Tallest statue	Chief Crazy Horse *(Thunderhead Mt., South Dakota)*	563 ft.
Highest bridge	Royal Gorge, Colorado	1,053 ft. above water
Longest suspension bridge	Verrazano Narrows, NY	4,250 ft
Longest steel arch bridge	New River Gorge, Fayetteville, Virginia	1,700 ft
Longest cantilever bridge	Commodore John Perry New Jersey/Pennsylvania	1,622 ft
Most damaging hurricane	Andrew *(1992)*	
Largest meteorite found	Canyon Diablo, Arizona	30 tons
Largest university	University of California	157,400 students
Largest library	Library of Congress, Washington DC	24,000,000 books
Busiest international airport	J.F. Kennedy International, New York	17,378,000 passengers a year
Busiest seaport	New York/New Jersey	
Busiest underground railway	New York Subway	1 trillion + *(passengers per year)*

WHAT TIME IS IT?

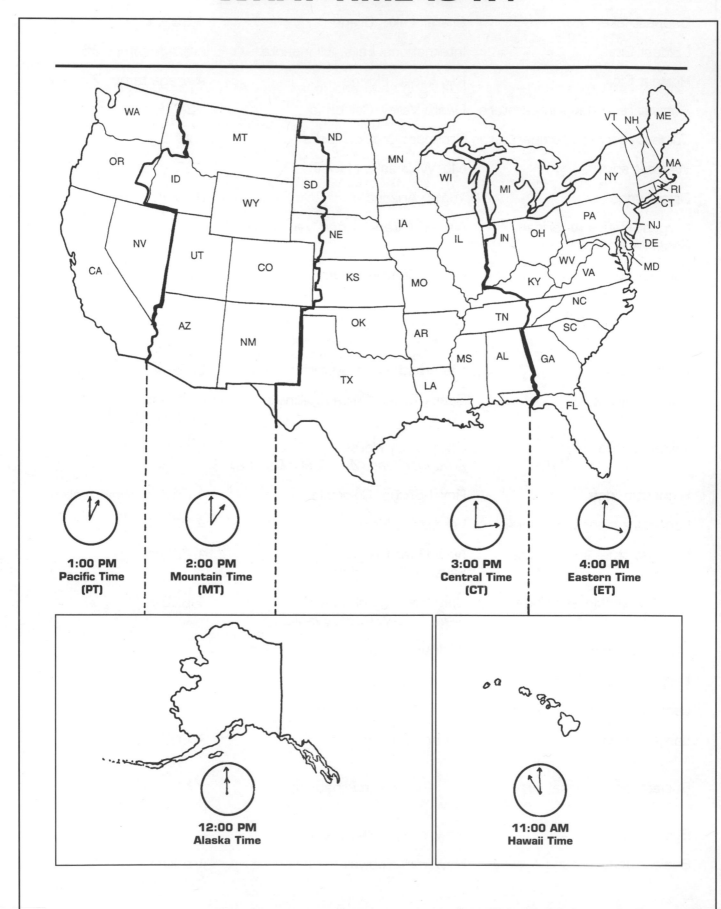

1:00 PM
Pacific Time
(PT)

2:00 PM
Mountain Time
(MT)

3:00 PM
Central Time
(CT)

4:00 PM
Eastern Time
(ET)

12:00 PM
Alaska Time

11:00 AM
Hawaii Time

U.S. Social Studies Yellow Pages, Rev. Ed.

GEOGRAPHY ABCs

Antarctic Circle — line of latitude at 66⅔° south latitude

Arctic Circle — line of latitude at 66⅔° north latitude

alluvial-soil deposits — soil made up of sand and mud deposited by flowing water

altitude — elevation

atlas — a collection of maps

Appalachian Highlands — a rugged region of several mountain ranges that extend from the northern tip of Maine southwest to Alabama

axis — an imaginary line running through the center of the earth between the North and South poles

basic — a large or small depression in the land surface

basin — a low, bowl-shaped landform surrounded by higher land

bay — an arm of a sea or lake extending into the land

butte — a small, flat-topped hill

Canadian Shield — a huge, horseshoe-shaped region that covers almost half of Canada; curves around Hudson Bay to the northern coast of Quebec

canal — a waterway dug across land for ships to pass between two larger bodies of water

canyon — a deep, narrow valley with steep sides formed by running water

cape — a point of land projecting into a sea or other body of water

capital — a city or town which is the seat of state or national government

cardinal directions — the four main geographic directions of north, south, east, and west

cartographer — a person who makes maps

census — a population count

climate — the pattern of weather in a certain place over a long period of time

coastal plain — plains found along the coasts of continents

compass rose — the symbol used on a map to show directions

continent — one of the seven largest landmasses of the world

contour map — a map that shows the elevation and landforms of an area

dam — a wall built across a river to slow or hold back the running water

degree — a unit of measurement of latitude and longitude

delta — a triangular section of land at the mouth of a river

desert climate zone — climate zones that are very dry and that have sparse plant life most of the year

economy — the way people use resources to meet their needs

elevation — height

equator — line of latitude which divides the earth into equal parts

exports — any goods that are sold to another nation

forest — a dense growth of trees covering a large area

geographer — a person who studies the earth and its life

geography — the study of the earth and of the ways people live and work on it

glacier — a large mass of ice that moves slowly over a land surface

grid — a set of lines used to find locations on a map

grid map — any map that is divided into squares labeled with a letter and number to help in location of places

hemisphere — half of the globe

gulf — a large area of sea or ocean that is partly surrounded by land

immigrant — a person who moves to a country other than the one where he/she is born

imports — goods that are brought into a country from another country

inland waterways — rivers, lakes, and canals

interior — the inland part of a country, away from the coasts and borders

interior plains — plains that are located away from the coasts of continents and that have a higher elevation than coastal plains

intermediate directions — northeast, northwest, southeast, and southwest

island — any body of land that is smaller than a continent and that is completely surrounded by water.

isthmus — a narrow piece of land that connects two larger masses of land

key — part of a map which tells the meaning of symbols; a legend

lake — a large inland body of fresh or salt water

landform — a feature of the earth's surface landmasses

latitude — lines on a map or globe that run east and west

legend — the part of a map that tells the meaning of symbols; a key

longitude — lines on a map or globe that run north and south

mesa — a big, flat landform that rises above surrounding land

mineral — any substance that is not of plant or animal origin

mountain — a landform that has steep slopes and some kind of peak or summit

mountain range — a chain of mountains

mouth — the place where a river empties into a large body of water

natural feature — a feature of the earth formed by nature, such as a waterfall, lake, mountain, or desert

natural resource — an element from the earth not made by man

ocean — a large body of salt water

parallel — a line of latitude on a map or globe

peninsula — a piece of land that extends from a continent and that is mostly surrounded by water

physical map — a map that shows how the land looks

plains — flat or gently rolling lands that are often less than 1,000 feet (305 meters) above sea level

plateau — a large area of flatland that is higher than the surrounding land and that has at least one steep side

political map — a map that shows how humans have divided the surface of the earth

population — all of the people who live in a specified area

prairie — an inland area that has thick, tall grasses covering soil that is usually fertile

precipitation — a deposit on the earth of rainfall or other moisture

Prime Meridian — the starting point for measuring longitude; runs through the Royal Observatory at Greenwich, England

region — an area of the world that shares some common characteristics

relief map — a map that shows the height of land above sea level

resource map — a map that shows the things found or produced in an area

river — a large natural stream of water that flows into an ocean, lake, etc.

river basin — land drained by a river

seaport — place where ships load and unload goods

scale — the calibrated line used on a map to indicate distance

sea level — average height of water in the world's oceans

society — a group of people bound by common culture and laws

special-purpose map — a map which gives one particular kind of information

superlative — of the highest order, quality, or degree

symbol — a drawing used on a map to represent something else

temperate — having mild or moderate climate

temperature — the measure of how hot or cold something is

time zone — division of the earth for the purpose of keeping time

tradition — a custom or belief passed from one generation to the next in a culture

tributary — a river or stream that flows into a larger river or stream

Tropic of Cancer — the parallel at $23\frac{1}{2}°$ N latitude

Tropic of Capricorn — the parallel at $23\frac{1}{2}°$ S latitude

valley — low-lying land between hills or ranges of mountains

volcano — an opening in the earth through which melted rock and other substances are forced out

waterfall — a natural stream of water descending from a height